CAN ANY GOOD THING COME FROM THE USA?

TESTIMONIALS OF SUCCESSFUL PEOPLE WHO KNOW THE VALUE OF PROCESS, POSITION AND PROFIT

VISIONARY DR. RENEE SUNDAY

© Sunday Publishing Company
Reneesunday.com
ISBN: 978-1-7334502-2-5

Table of Contents

List of Authors

Can Anything Good Come From New York City?

Brenda Sawyer

Brenda Sawyer was born and raised in New York City and currently resides in Philadelphia. Her strong spiritual foundation acknowledges that she is a Woman of God who believes that she can do all things through Christ who strengthens her. As a young child, Brenda has always had a passion for teaching and imparting knowledge. After graduating from Hunter College with a dual major in Psychology and Early Childhood

3

Education, Brenda taught elementary school for twenty-six years for the School District of Philadelphia. Brenda holds a second Master's degree from Cabrini College. In addition to being a published author of Encouraging Words For The Mind, Spirit And Soul, she is also the Founder and CEO of GIRLS WALKING WITH INTEGRITY EMPOWERING FOR DESTINY (GWWI), a Christian mentoring ministry which empowers young ladies between the ages of eight and eighteen to become all that God has called them to be.

You may connect with Brenda Sawyer at:

www.brendasawyer.com

www.girlswalkingwithintegrity.com

www.facebook.com/brendasawyer.58

www.instagram.com/brendasawyerencourages

CAN ANYTHING GOOD COME FROM NEW YORK CITY?

Yes, my name is Brenda Sawyer and I am that good thing. I was born and raised in Astoria, Queens New York City Housing Projects. I came from an intact Christian family comprised of my father, my mother and my older brother. We were a "closely-knit" family, always having fun and going places together. We had a great deal of love and respect for one another. My parents always taught us the values and morals of treating people the way we want to be treated. Most importantly, they taught us to respect the elders and our peers.

Unfortunately, this respect was not always reciprocated to me by some of my peers (classmates). For the most part, my classmates and I got along well with each other. However, I can recall two girls from the projects who did not get along with me at all, no matter how hard I tried to make friends with them.

They would bully me during and after school. They

would team up together to pull my braids, call me names, punch me, step all over my new shoes and even try to take my lunch money for no reason at all. I could never understand why they did all that since we lived in the same neighborhood and our parents were friends. It made absolutely no sense whatsoever and the bullying continued every day from third grade up until fifth grade.

I was being jumped and beaten up while walking home from school and didn't want to tell my teacher for fear of something worse happening to me. Every day, I came home from school not wanting to return. My parents were quite concerned and asked me to explain what was going on. Finally, when I told them, they wanted to meet with the girls' parents to discuss the matter. After the discussion, the bullying subsided for about a week and went on again. At this point, my parents advised me to ignore them and to bring it to the teacher's attention the next time it happened.

When I told my teacher, much to my surprise she brushed it aside, she ignored me and did nothing to resolve the issue. I didn't understand why this kept

6

happening and why an adult would allow it. My parents made a decision to discuss the matter with the school's principal but to no avail. It seemed as though no one wanted to solve or address the problem.

I remember praying one night and asking God to forgive my enemies and to protect me from them. I know that prayer works because the bullying stopped by the end of the fifth-grade school year and we eventually became friends. Interesting enough, we found out that we had so much more in common than we knew.

As my life began to unfold and I became much more matured in my thinking, I knew that God had a greater plan for my life. (Jeremiah 29:11) I believe that He allowed me to be bullied so that I could become the nurturing and caring teacher that I aspired to be at the age of five. It made me the strong survivor that I am today. It also made me develop a greater love and passion for teaching elementary school, where I could implement conflict resolution in my classroom whenever my students had problems with each other. I helped them to resolve their differences by having them discuss the issues, not ignore them and "sweeping them under the carpet."

I set out to be the best teacher that God had called me to be, by genuinely caring about them and by always trying to be there for them when they needed someone to talk to. My goal is to teach from a heart of love and respect and to make a difference in their lives.

The cost of
starting over is being
willing to let go.

Guy Finley

Can Anything Good Come Out Of Arkansas?

DR. ONIKA SHIRLEY

Dr. Onika L. Shirley, the founder and CEO of Action Speaks Volume, Inc. is an International Confidence and Procrastination Coach and Motivational Speaker. She is the former President of the Greater Memphis Chapter of NAPW for almost 5 years. Dr. O is the Founder and Director of Action Speaks Volume Orphanage Home in India and Founder and Director of Action Speaks Volume Sewing School in Pakistan. She is author, master storyteller, Radio host of Action Takers

Walking by Faith Live radio broadcast, and serial entrepreneur. Dr. Onika L. Shirley is a mother and proud grandmother to baby Aubrey which is her everything.

CAN ANYTHING GOOD COME OUT OF ARKANSAS?

This is a question that many have asked but my response has always been – come and see. People have asked this question all through the years and people still ask the same question today.

God is a God of hope and He uses whom He desires to use for His glory. I heard and I believe what He says is true and it's true all the time. How is it that God is speaking to us today? Who is God choosing to use today and where is she from?

God is speaking to His people through His Holy word, and through people like me that He has placed in the state of Arkansas to do kingdom work all over the world. Sometimes the most difficult things to see are the ones right before our eyes. We are overlooked because of where we live or where we were raised and it becomes very easy to lose sight of what seems to be obvious. The story that people tell themselves about Arkansas, and perhaps about their birthplace too, blinds them to the truth that is right in front of

14

them. The things we hear and say about certain people and places are just the compilation of a scene within a story and it is told from an individual's point of view. Over the years, I have learned that no point of view sees everything. The story people tell about Arkansas might be wrong – can anything good come out of Arkansas?

The world is divided to a point that good things and good people can come from anywhere. Does anything good come from Arkansas? Of course, it does, because I am here and to be honest there are so many other people and good things that have been in Arkansas even before I got here. I am just one of the good things that came from Arkansas. When people think they know a place, it makes them think they know everyone living there and they know what they are capable of, however, that is usually wrong and I'm living proof. There are good things I have to offer God's kingdom, God has opened the door for me to make a difference in the lives of a lot of people around the world through my social media presence and by serving as an adoptive and

15

foster parent for the state of Arkansas for more than a decade. My main goal is to inspire others to unwrap their gifts, build unshakable confidence, and to live by faith in God. I want to see people not just moved but transformed. It is very important to me to reach out and help people who are suffering and hurting. I have made it one of the main focuses of Action Speaks Volume, Inc. I do not only want to share inspirational messages via social media as to how faithful God is, I also want to show people how faithful He is in practical ways. I have personally sacrificed from my household budget and allocated income to help the less fortunate through world mission initiatives. Over the years, my giving has been incremental. I have helped people in countries all around the world (India, Pakistan, and the continent of Africa).

The more I give to world missions, the more I desire to help those who can't help themselves. World missions has been a passion of mine for years, I started out with donating to a television ministry every month for several years. I have also donated on a regular basis to organizations like Feed the Children and the Mid-South Foodbank of Memphis, TN. God always makes a way

16

and I thank him for the opportunities he has given me to help and serve more people. My motto is "Walk by Faith and Serve the Kingdom of God." God gives seed to the sower and she is from Arkansas.

We are what we imagine.
Our very existence consists
in our imagination of ourselves.
The greatest tragedy that can
befall us is to go unimagined.

N. Scott Momaday

Can Anything Good Come From Gainesville, Florida?

Divine Healing Ministries

Prophetess Charlotte Ellis - Colbert

Charlotte Colbert was born in Gainesville, FL and has two wonderful parents, Earnest Ellis Jr. and Gladys Simmons Ellis, a brother (Napoleon), and sister (Kim) of whom she loves greatly.

Charlotte loves to sing and discovered that gift at an early age. While growing up, Charlotte would sit for hours listening to the songs her mom and aunts would

21

sing. The Infamous, "Simmons Sisters," played an intrinsic part in her love for singing. Charlotte has been blessed to grace the stage and complete studio time and recordings for, Gospel greats such as, Minister Beverly Crawford, Minister Steve Lawrence, Bishop T.D.Jakes, Karen-Clark Sheard, Vicki Winans, Marvin Sapp and Dorinda Clark Cole. Charlotte and her mother completed their first live recording and are in the process of working diligently to release their songs to the public. As with everything in life, unforeseen roadblocks have hindered the process of time but not the promises of God.

Charlotte received her bachelor's degree from Tuskegee University and utilizes every moment as a teachable moment for herself and family.

She discovered her ability to express herself through writing at a young age. She has copy right to songs, poems, and short stories she has written. Her desire and hunger is to reveal to others how to live a successful life in face of adversity or transition. She was honored to contribute to the book, Manifestation Now as a co-author, in which she received the title of best-selling author.

The need to help others run deep in her veins. Her compassion for others is an understatement. Charlotte finds great solace working with in the ministry, Divine Healing Ministry that was founded by her mother, Evangelist Gladys Ellis. She understands that a small twist of fate could have her on the receiving end instead of fulling the duty and honor of giving.

She has been married for 23 years, to Dwan Colbert Sr., is mother to three dynamic children, Dwan Colbert Jr., Taylor Colbert, and Jaden Colbert. She finds herself in constant awe of their strength, balance and many achievements. The order of importance for Charlotte, is, God, family and her continued quest for greatness.

Proverbs 31:17- She girds herself with strength. And strengthens her arms.

Evangelist Gladys Ellis

Evangelist Gladys Simmons-Ellis is from Monteocha, which is a rural community outside the city limit of Gainesville, FL. She was saved at an early age and started her great works for God's kingdom. God called her into the ministry, and she answered "Yes, Lord". She was ordained in the Church of God by Faith in

1999. She is a member of Jerusalem Church of God by Faith (Monteocha) and currently serves under the pastoral leadership of Elder Duane E. Gainey.

Evangelist Ellis was born into a large family. Her parents, the late Andy and Shellie Simmons had 10 children, (8 girls and 2 boys). The family could not afford many material items, but their family base and foundation were that of love, compassion and God. The Simmons Family was gifted with musical talents that lead to she and her sisters forming, The Simmons Sisters gospel group. Being a part of The Simmons Sisters Gospel group prepared Evangelist Ellis for a life of spreading the Gospel through song, preaching and teaching the incomparable word of the Lord.

Evangelist Ellis has been married to her husband, Earnest Ellis for 50 years and they have two adult children, Napoleon Ellis and Charlotte Ellis Colbert. Her second ministry is her love and devotion to her family. She is a proud grand mother and is care giver to her eldest sister. She is the constant figure that bonds her family together.

Evangelist Ellis was fortunate to work for Shands hospital as a surgical technologist for 47 years. Not only did she exemplify Christ in the community and with her family, but she also exemplified Christ in the workplace.

Evangelist Ellis is known for spreading the gospel through song and through her teaching. She carries the word in her heart and lives Psalms 34 "I will bless the Lord at all times and his praise shall continually be in my mouth." She is exceptional and an inspirational fixture in the City of Gainesville. She has devoted a lifetime to community service and the development of programs that contributes to the well-being of others. Evangelist Ellis is Founder of Divine Healing Ministries. A Ministry that provides clothing, food and shelter for single mothers and their families.

It is evident that Evangelist Ellis seeks the Lord daily. Through her ministry, lives have been saved and recommitted to Christ. She is a true warrior for God! Proverbs 31:30 says, "Charm is deceitful, and beauty is vain, but a woman who fears the Lord, shall bepraised."

26

Can Any Good Come from Gainesville, Florida?
Divine Healing Ministries

The current state of the world is that of worry, fear, lack, uncertainty, pain, and doubt. Disasters are happening all over the world, some parts of the world are plagued with locust, while other parts have recently experienced drought, unusual flooding, bushfires, mudslides, volcano eruptions and a host of other unexplainable events. The world as we know it today is changing and transcending in ways that will eventually cause us to live life with parameters identified as "The New Normal." The latest pandemic that the world is facing is coronavirus (Covid-19). It is currently unknown how this disease spreads, how people are getting infected and the best computer model predicts that 100,000 to 200,000 Americans will die from Covid-19 during the upcoming months, even if the country continues strict social distancing measures. With severe job loss across the globe, surmounting deaths and homelessness, there is still some good in the world. There are still people who genuinely care and a host of individuals who believe that by providing hope and

27

lending a helping hand during a time of stress, rids fear, worry and doubt while simultaneously propelling us to the other side of struggle and life's pain. Often, when we think of something being good, or referenced as good, we tend to automatically equate it with an abundance of money, the purchase of high-end things or social acceptance. In taking time to look far beyond what the human eyes can see, the good that still exists is that of kindness, love, gentleness, faithfulness, and humility. So, when the question is asked, "What Good Can Come from Gainesville, FL?"

The true answer is the gift of humanity. The good that comes from Gainesville, FL is extended through the mother-daughter duo, Evangelist Gladys Ellis and her daughter, author and songwriter, Charlotte Colbert. Just the same way there is darkness in the world, there is also light. **According to Matthew 5:16, "In the same way, let your light shine before others, that they may see your good deeds and glorify your Father in heaven."** Due to the desire and urge to replace darkness with light and also offer good instead of evil, Divine Healing Ministries was birthed.

Evangelist Gladys Ellis grew up in the rural farm community of Monteocha, FL, just minutes away from the Gainesville, FL city line. She was blessed to have been raised by two hardworking parents who instilled humility, service, and unwavering love for the body of Christ. While her parents were not fortunate enough to obtain a formal education, they taught Evangelist Ellis and her nine siblings (7 sisters and two brothers) the importance of education, hard work and how to have compassion for others. Evangelist Ellis and her family did not have all their needs provided, yet, they were rich in love, respect for one another and support. Upbringing during the civil rights movement taught her at an early age not to compromise her love for GOD in moments of unrest, uncertainty, and despair. At the age of eight, Evangelist started what would become a lifelong journey of Ministry with a servant's heart.

Coming from a family that has a musical background, Evangelist Gladys Ellis and her sisters started a singing group (The Simmons Sisters). This made them travel all over Florida opening for Gospel artists such as the Williams Brothers, the Gospel Keynotes, Shirley Caesar,

The Mighty Clouds of Joy and the Truthettes. Singing was therapeutic and it was practiced constantly in her home and church life. Evangelist was blessed with the opportunity to participate in play rights such as, Black Voices and during these times of Ministry, she knew there was a greater call on her life to do more, to give more, and to share the gifts that God has bestowed upon her.

The journey has not always been easy and at times, Evangelist Ellis wonders where she would have been if she did not embrace God's love, direction, and instructions for her life. Growing up in southern Florida during a time of hate, conflict, extreme hardship, and racism, she had to work hard. As a child, she did not have the luxury of playing with barbie dolls, playing dress-up or make-believe. At the tender age of five, she had already started working. Her father was a sharecropper and before school, Evangelist Ellis and her siblings had to work in a tobacco field picking tobacco and grinding sugar cane. After the morning work was completed, she and her siblings would trolley on to school for formal learning. Upon returning home from school, the tobacco field was the place of destination to complete another cycle of chores that included picking peas and shucking corn. Taking planned time off, sick leave or family leave was not an option.

The only option was to work. She could have allowed the harshness of that time to stain her view of life and people. The need to work and support the family could have allowed her to bottle feelings of resentment and bitterness. Even at that young age, she searched for acts of kindness for the common good. Evangelist Ellis experienced the hardship of growing up in the south. A visit to the hospital normally led to a waiting area in which one side was labeled for colored and the other for whites.

The chains of inequality and constant reminders of not being good enough hovered over her entire childhood. She learned how to take the remnants of unfairness and move beyond to offer a better good. She refused to allow the harshness of that time to distort her view of life and people. Little did she know, seeds of overcoming obstacles were planted with each injustice, each day in the tobacco field and each time her young body needed rest, but she had to keep moving and pressing forward.

Philippians 1:6; "being confident of this that He who began a good work in you will carry it on to completion until the day of Christ Jesus." I John 4:16, And so we know and rely on the love God has for us. God is love. Whoever lives in love lives in God, and God in them.

When Evangelist became an adult, she married Earnest Ellis and had two children, Napoleon and Charlotte Ellis. Her devotion to her husband and children is indescribable. The order for her life continues in the following order of God, family, and Ministry. To humbly submit your will for that of someone else's is hard for a lot of people to do. Becoming a wife and mother came with a multitude of challenges, yet another phase of her life continued to shape and sharpen the very core of her existence. With every trial, success and hardship, Evangelist Ellis continued to ask a question, what good can come from this? There was never a moment when she did not believe that all things, the good, the bad and indifferent were working for her good.

Even with her devotion to family and love for God, she still faced obstacles that delivered feelings of fear, worry and stress. These feelings alone can paralyze good thoughts and defer dreams. Each time she was faced with these emotions, she turned to God. In 1992, Evangelist suffered from bell's palsy, which has been characterized as a weakness in facial muscle that causes half of the face to droop. The recovery time is approximately six months, but due to her strong faith in God, she knew without a shadow of doubt that God would heal her and strengthen the compromised muscle. During that walk of faith, she remained prayerful, continued singing songs of worship, and never doubted the power of God. Her life for a moment had changed but her position in God never wavered. She went from drinking from a cup to now drinking through a straw. Her ability to sing was now restricted and she was limited to sing through the corner of her mouth. That restriction did not stop her from praising God. Bells' Palsy affected the Evangelist on a Thursday and the following Wednesday,

God healed and restored total use of her facial muscles. Her standard song of worship during that time was, "Because He Lives, I Can Face Tomorrow" Deliverance, healing and a renewed faith in God is the good that came out from this light affliction.

Just as Job said, "that which I fear the most has come upon me!" Evangelist went through seasons of having a "Job Experience!" **(Job 3:25 What I feared has come upon me; what I dreaded has happened to me).** She had to encourage herself during the storm, believing that something good will be the result of the struggle. Within the sanctum of her soul, she continued to reflect on the times when God was always and continues to be a bridge over troubled water.

He is faithful and just to watch over His word. She always rejoiced over witnessing the miracles He performed in the lives of others and often praised God as if it were her miracle. Therefore, in assurance, she agrees with the writer who sang, "Though trials come on every hand, I feel like going on." The justice of God showed forth his goodness! This experience and every other experience propelled Evangelist into a greater work in which she became a minister and pushed harder to accomplish significant works for the kingdom of God. During this time, the call to give more of herself kept growing, and as years past, the need to help others grew more intense. From that yearning in the spirit, Divine Healing Ministries was born.

As mentioned above, Evangelist Ellis has a daughter, Charlotte Colbert. Charlotte works side by side in the Ministry with her mother. They both have a close relationship, and the way Charlotte loves and honors God is an absolute result of the life Evangelist Ellis lived before the family. The word of God consistently flowed through the lips of Evangelist Ellis but most importantly, she was an example and a beacon of light that her children and husband needed. For the Good; do all things really work? Is there anything Good that can come out of America? Of all we see in the earth today, this question holds great weight for the human side of an individual to ask. If you understand that by spirit, then you know all that God created, He called good and very good. Charlotte has always had an analytical mind, would question the "why is" and the "how's." There were many things that her mother Evangelist Gladys Ellis was able to tell her from experience and while growing, she learned to embrace that wisdom.

She instilled a no matter what, "have Faith in the Lord, and trust in Him. "That principle was also imparted into her children. Although Charlotte has seen many works of the family, she needed to find the light that would illuminate the path to her purpose in life.

As children, we dream of the life we desire to have, which are illussioned by things we see on television, people, and the imagination within ourselves. The more Charlotte grew, the more her ideas, desires, and aspirations continued to grow. She had seen the path of her parents and the way of righteousness, and that was a route that her heart desired. Charlotte developed an interest to know who she was, to find her identity, and to know her place in the world. She no longer wanted to be engulfed in the shadow of her parents and yearned to experience more of what God mapped out for her footsteps. Preparations to set markers in life was established. Always remembering that the key to succession is to keep God first, she took a big leap of faith and journeyed to Tuskegee, Alabama where she attended and became a graduate of Tuskegee University. She came from a family who lived by spiritual principles, and though those principles followed her, there was a part of her that knew mistakes would happen; but still, the Love of God filtered and accompanied her. (You, Lord, are forgiving and good abounding in love to all who call to you. Psalms 86:5) While attending Tuskegee University, there were trials from financial hardships that would lead to a line of frustration. Even with two working parents, making tuition payments was a challenge.

What had been imparted in her had to be exercised in such a way that the results showed an outward manifestation, by way of what was an inner covenant of the purpose for her life. God who never fails, worked it out. There were still challenges while pursuing her education, but because she had faith, separation from

37

her faith was not an option. Survival was the only option and to wallow in sorrow was not the portal that would lead her to the supplier. She witnessed her mother pray and sing or make melody in her heart. It was the cry in her spirit that got the attention of the Heavenlies. It did not matter what the financial aid office had on their books. She only knew what God had in mind and that was for her to graduate from Tuskegee University. God is a God of miracles and His word is final.

While at home for summer break, Charlotte was robbed at gunpoint. Her possessions were stolen, and her friend received twelve stiches across his forehead from being hit over the head with the butt of the gun. During that quick moment of darkness, all she did was hold on to the name of Jesus. At that moment, her faith was not shaken because she knew that God would spare their lives. That experience should have left her riddled with fear and plagued with anxiety but, she refused to let evil win. Instead, she asked the same question, what good can come out of this? The good that came out of that experience was a testimony. Evil knocked, but God answered the door. The Good that came from this was God's constant hand molding her for greater works. Page after Page became chapters in her life, finally, she graduated from Tuskegee University with a bachelor's degree in education. The reason for sharing different milestones in the lives of Evangelist Ellis and Charlotte Colbert is with the hope that someone reading this will be inspired to have faith, choose love and to never give up.

And two become one! Charlotte met her husband, Dwan Colbert Sr. while in college. They became one in the Union of Marriage with three amazing children. Two of their children are in college, and the other is in middle school. There is no perfect marriage and in Marriage, there MUST be a common ground of forgiveness and new ways to show love. NO marriage is the same...Every Marriage has Different Issues...Some Days you are Happy...Some Days you May want to choke each other and Some issues are more Stressful than others...But through it all, each party has to invite God in and ask Him to stay. With each challenge in her marriage, God continues to mold Charlotte through her experiences.

Evangelist Gladys Ellis and Charlotte had to experience the ups and downs of life. Through their hunger to please God while searching for ways to help others, Divine Healing Ministries has been very instrumental. Divine Healing Ministry is a ministry that was founded on the foundation of truth by the word of God; to restore the Ministry of healing and reconciliation; not just to the church but to the nations. The Ministry helps hurting people during a time when they need support as they enter a different phase of life to overcome obstacles while striving for change and a better life. The desire to serve others is commendable, yet Evangelist Ellis and Charlotte understand that nothing happens without God. All that they experienced has not been in vain. The experiences were necessary, on purpose and were beneficial in the development of their character and hearts to have compassion for others.

Good can come out of the USA, good can come out from Gainesville, Florida, but most importantly, something good can come out of Divine Healing Ministries.

Money and things of this world receive a lot of accolades and frankly, society tends to recognize greatness based on how much money you have, how many cars you have, how many "likes" you can attain and social staging. By allowing the Fruits of the Spirit to take total control, the Ministry offers a greater good by helping others during a bleak time in their lives. Although the Ministry helps people throughout the year, the mother-daughter duo begins every year seeking for families or individuals to show acts of kindness, love, and support. In the spirit of humility, they humble themselves knowing that it is God that worketh both the will and the ability to do. In November of every year, the mother-daughter duo prepares an evening of worship by honoring the community. This worship experience affords them the opportunity to be of service to those in need. With the support from yearly donations, the Ministry takes every donation received and bless people of the community with the means necessary to provide rent payments, a place to live, home furnishing, clothes, dinners, plane tickets back to an original destination and many more. Evangelist Ellis and Charlotte know that they are chosen vessels placed on a divine journey

41

ordered by God. Every personal experience they encountered was preparing them to take on the responsibility of giving everything good about themselves. We are in the time when God is here to show up; while He uses us to show forth who He is for us to see the light of God spew forth from our lives. As children of God, we must always remember that if we place God first, then secondary things will not be suppressed.

They continue to share the gospel of the Kingdom. Preaching and teaching the word of God; singing until deliverance takes place, they do it in such a way that God is glorified in all they do.

Ephesians 3:20-21, Now to him who is able to do immeasurably more than all we ask or imagine, according to his power that is at work within us. 21 to him be glory in the church and in Christ Jesus throughout all generations, for ever and ever! Amen.

The mother-daughter duo of Evangelist Gladys Ellis and Author/Songwriter, Charlotte Colbert is just a small channel of the Good that can come from the USA, Gainesville, FL and Divine Healing Ministries.

Always do right. This will gratify some people and astonish the rest.

Mark Twain

Can Anything Good Come From Birmingham?

DR. RENEE SUNDAY

From poverty to purpose, Dr. Renee Sunday created a seller career. Empowering and educating, this ordained minister serves in media, business development, and healthcare. As a Board-Certified Anesthesiologist for nineteen years, she's been voted as one of the top 100 in the nation.

Can Anything Good Come From Birmingham?

Ever heard of a city or neighborhood that was given a bad rep? Have you ever heard of a street name and immediately associated it with something negative? It could be drugs, gangs, poverty, racism, teen pregnancy, or even poor education. Matter of fact, you can merely read the words right now of Compton or The Bronx or Atlanta. And depending on where you're from or where you are in the world, your response may not be as favorable. Even if you consider places like Qatar or Iraq, you may immediately associate them with war and death and militant overtakes.

It's true that there are some placed in the world with a horrible reputation, but amazing people form there. Have you ever considered that there are very real people in these places? Outside of the statistics, outside of the headlines, outside of rumors – there is some good in everything that's seemingly bad. Indeed, many of us are living proof that that not everything or everyone, which comes out of a presumably corrupt region, is automatically destined for failure or demise.

47

And there's one city in particular that has had not so favorable characteristics in the past; yet it has produced one of the greatest and most selfless human beings every. That city is Birmingham, Alabama. And there's a woman named *Dr. Renee Sunday* who is proof that something good CAN come out of Birmingham. But what, supposedly, is so bad about Birmingham?

For starters, it's ranked high in crime. In 2016 it was deemed to be #12 on the list of dangerous cities. It was also listed as being #25 for the most murders in the entire United States. In 2015, it came in at #39 for the worst school system quality. And sadly, Alabama has always ranked as one of the poorest states in the country. It is said that more than 1 in 4 children there live in poverty. And while all of these, and more, are facts about Birmingham, there are other truths that not many want to accept. Even in the midst of chaos, something can emerge that is beautiful and powerful, something that goes against statistics. That's where you have to be reminded of one intelligent and innovative woman.

Dr. Renee Sunday was born to very humble beginnings,

but in a home of structure and love. Education was very important and respect was always exemplified. While money was not always available, hard work was always implemented and Dr. Renee was destined for greatness because of it. However, her school life wasn't always fair.

By the time Dr. Sunday was in her teen years, she had experienced a "not so pretty side" of life. In school, she was given the nickname of "Olive Oil" and was a victim of bullying. She was very tall and thin, often being picked on because of it. Due to the cruelty of those around her, she dealt with low self-esteem and constant nagging from her peers. It appears that they would purposely find something wrong with her, mocking her physical appearance and everything about her. She simply didn't seem to fit in. But because of what was instilled in her, she kept going.

Eventually, this gave her a deep love and respect for people. She recognized that the world needed more of what some failed to give her – compassion, respect, and positivity. This gave her fuel to do just that.

She completed high school, went on to college, and pursued an intentional education in the medicinal field. She learned lessons, had trials, dealt with grief, and even battled with perfectionism. Yes, she wanted everything to be perfect and all of the time. However, the world that we live in doesn't quite work that way. And one day, in her adult years, Dr. Renee Sunday had to experience just how imperfect the world was. She learned a hard lesson in inevitability. She learned that it doesn't matter how prepared you are, things can shift – either for you or against you. And the biggest lesson she learned was that a 6-figure salary could be taken in the blink of an eye.

As a Board Certified Anesthesiologist, Dr. Sunday experienced the economic crash of 2008 in an unprecedented way. She enjoyed her patients, she was making strides in the community, and she loved what she was doing. But in an instant, that salary was taken from her when she was laid off. It was then that this intelligent woman from Birmingham realized it was time for a change. It was time to believe in the Birmingham within.

Yes, her roots were deep and she has always been

proud of who and what she was. But she had to step up and step out. And this means she had to go back to those lessons she learned as a little girl in her parents' home. She had to go back to the lessons of strength and resilience that she encountered as a Birmingham teenager. Indeed, she had to tap into the insight received during her days in church and school.

Therefore, This mature woman had to become the best part of Birmingham. And what was that? That was Dr. Renee Sunday, the risk taker.

You see, the very thing that most said couldn't come out of Birmingham did just that. Where there was nothing but poverty and despair, Dr. Renee Sunday used the lessons of her childhood and created her own economy. She tapped inside of the gifts within and became what the people of her youth said she'd never be. She became herself – unapologetically.

Today, she is a best selling author and keynote speaker that successfully runs and operates Sunday Publishing, the Sunday Foundation, and Good Deeds Media

Network. She is also a Media Consulting Coach, an ordained Minister, and a world traveler. A true humanitarian, she gets her inspiration from serving others and pouring into them. Her innate gift is to help others dig deep within and become who they were created to be. Additionally, she was named to the list of the Top 100 Anesthesiologists in the United States multiple times. Her accolades and experience are extensive. The lives that she has touched are immeasurable. But beyond that, the stigma that she has killed is undeniable.

Dr. Renee Sunday could have been one of those people who grew up in poverty and stayed there; but she wasn't! She could have been one of those who didn't receive a proper education; but she wasn't! She could have been a minority female placed in the judicial system and destined for "death row" statistics; but she wasn't! Instead, she was and is a pioneer.

She was and is an influencer. She was and is a destiny pusher. She was, is, and will forever be Dr. Renee Sunday.

So, can anything good come from Birmingham? The answer is an emphatic, "YES!" Because out of Birmingham is a Rickey Smiley, there was a Helen Keller, there is a Ruben Studdard, there is a Condoleezza Rice, there is a Carl Lewis, and there is a Dr. Renee Sunday – a woman of many hats and many successes.

Can Any Good Thing

When one door of
happiness closes, another
opens; but often we look so
long at the closed door that
we do not see the one that
has opened for us.

Helen Keller

Encouraging Quotes

Let others lead small lives,
but not you. Let others
argue over small things,
but not you. Let others cry
over small hurts, but not you.
Let others leave their
future in someone else's
hands, but not you.
Jim Rohn

Trust yourself,
then you will know
how to live.
Johann Wolfgang van Goethe

You can never
cross the ocean
unless you have the
courage to lose
sight of the shore.
André Gide

When one door of
happiness closes, another
opens; but often we look
so long at the closed
door that we do not
see the one that
has opened for us.
Helen Keller

It is our choices
that show what we
truly are, far more
than our abilities.
J.K. Rowling

I'm not afraid...
I was BORN for this!
Joan of Arc

Whatever you are
willing to put up with is
exactly what you will have.
Anonymous

There is a fire inside.
Sit down beside it. Watch
the flames, the ancient,
flickering dance of yourself.
John MacEnulty

Destiny is not a
matter of chance, it is a
matter of choice. It is not a
thing to be waited for, it is a
thing to be achieved.
William Jennings Bryan

I have always known
that at last I would take
this road, but yesterday I
did not know that it would
be today.
Japanese Haiku

Notes

Notes

Can Any Good Thing

Notes

Can Any Good Thing

Notes

Can Any Good Thing

Notes

Can Any Good Thing

Notes

Can Any Good Thing

Notes

Can Any Good Thing

Notes

Can Any Good Thing

Notes

Can Any Good Thing

Notes

Can Any Good Thing

Notes

Can Any Good Thing

Notes

Can Any Good Thing

Notes

Can Any Good Thing

Notes

Can Any Good Thing

Notes

Can Any Good Thing

Notes

Can Any Good Thing

Notes

Can Any Good Thing

Notes

Can Any Good Thing

Notes

Can Any Good Thing

Notes

Can Any Good Thing

Notes

Can Any Good Thing

www.ingramcontent.com/pod-product-compliance
Lightning Source LLC
Chambersburg PA
CBHW031223090426
42740CB00007B/690